NEW VANGUARD 235

KATYUSHA

Russian Multiple Rocket Launchers
1941–Present

JAMIE PRENATT　　　　ILLUSTRATED BY ADAM HOOK

First published in Great Britain in 2016 by Osprey Publishing,
PO Box 883, Oxford, OX1 9PL, UK
1385 Broadway, 5th Floor, New York, NY 10018, USA
E-mail: info@ospreypublishing.com

Osprey Publishing, part of Bloomsbury Publishing Plc

© 2016 Osprey Publishing Ltd.

All rights reserved. Apart from any fair dealing for the purpose of private study, research, criticism or review, as permitted under the Copyright, Designs and Patents Act, 1988, no part of this publication may be reproduced, stored in a retrieval system, or transmitted in any form or by any means, electronic, electrical, chemical, mechanical, optical, photocopying, recording or otherwise, without the prior written permission of the copyright owner. Inquiries should be addressed to the Publishers.

A CIP catalog record for this book is available from the British Library

Print ISBN: 978 1 4728 1086 1
PDF ebook ISBN: 978 1 4728 1087 8
ePub ebook ISBN: 978 1 4728 1088 5

Index by Fionbar Lyons
Typeset in Sabon and Myriad Pro
Originated by PDQ Media, Bungay, UK
Printed in China through World Print Ltd

16 17 18 19 20   10 9 8 7 6 5 4 3 2 1

Osprey Publishing supports the Woodland Trust, the UK's leading woodland conservation charity. Between 2014 and 2018 our donations will be spent on their Centenary Woods project in the UK.

www.ospreypublishing.com

ACKNOWLEDGMENTS

The author would like to thank Mr George T. Norris for his gracious assistance.

Cover photo is courtesy of the Central Museum of the Armed Forces, Moscow via Stavka (www.stavka.org.uk)

CONTENTS

ORIGINS — 4
- Early rockets
- Russian rocketry and the first MRLs

WORLD WAR II MRLs — 8
- BM-13
- BM-8
- M-28
- M-30
- BM-31-12
- Organization
- Production

OPERATIONAL USE — 18

COLD WAR AND MODERN MRLs — 24
- BM-24
- BM-14 and RPU-14
- BMD-20
- BM-25 Korshun (Kite)
- BM-21 Grad (Hail)
- 9P140 Uragan (Hurricane)
- TOS-1 Buratino (Pinocchio)/TOS-1A Solntsepek (Sun)
- 9A52 Smerch (Whirlwind)

ASSOCIATED EQUIPMENT — 45

SELECT BIBLIOGRAPHY — 47

INDEX — 48

KATYUSHA

RUSSIAN MULTIPLE ROCKET LAUNCHERS 1941–PRESENT

ORIGINS

Early rockets
The details of the appearance of the first primitive rocket – probably in China – are obscure, as the Chinese term means "fire arrow" and incendiary arrows fired from bows were widely used by the Chinese. By the 13th century, however, the existence of a military rocket can be clearly established. The advantages of firing rockets, in this case rocket-propelled arrows, en masse were quickly identified and Chinese manuscripts contain several early designs for multiple rocket launchers (MRLs) that were capable of firing up to 100 of these projectiles. The Koreans also fielded such a device, the *hwacha* or "fire cart," against Japan in the 1500s.

The growth of the Mongol Empire undoubtedly helped spread rocket technology throughout Asia, the Arab world, and to Europe, where military rockets were used in combat in the late 1300s. By the 1600s, military rocketry was well known in Europe.

In India, military rockets were in common use by the 1700s and the Kingdom of Mysore established a rocket artillery force of some 5,000 men. It introduced the use of a cylindrical metal case for the rocket body, giving it far greater strength than earlier rockets. Although still rudimentary, these rockets were used to good effect during Mysore's conflicts with the British, most notably at the battle of Seringapatam in 1792.

The British experience in Mysore and its capture of almost 10,000 rockets led to increased interest in military rockets in Europe. Recognizing the inherent advantages of rockets and inspired by the examples captured in

> **ROCKETS VERSUS GUNS**
> Rockets have a number of important advantages over guns as artillery weapons. They are lighter and more mobile, the rocket cases can be made thinner and can contain relatively more payload than artillery shells, because they are subject to less stress on firing, and rockets can achieve long ranges without a corresponding increase in firing platform weight. In addition, the large warheads, combined with the ability to fire many rockets near-simultaneously, produce an important psychological shock effect on the enemy.
>
> Accuracy, at least until the advent of modern course-corrected rockets and smart submunitions, was poor, although using rockets en masse could compensate for this shortcoming. In addition, rocket launchers place a greater demand on the logistics system for ammunition resupply than conventional artillery.

India, the British inventor Sir William Congreve set about designing what would become the first modern military rocket. He improved and standardized the individual components – including the propellant – which facilitated production and, more importantly, resulted in higher quality rockets. The 1804 Congreve rocket became an accepted and regularly used tool in military operations. It was actually a family of rockets, weighing from 6 to 300 pounds and with several types of explosive and non-explosive payloads, which could be fired from ground and naval mounts. For guidance, it relied on a long and cumbersome stick attached to the side or, later, the base of the rocket's body.

Another British inventor, William Hale, introduced the next major technological innovation in rocketry. Research had demonstrated that the accuracy of projectiles was much greater if they were spun in flight. Hale applied this principle to rockets, and in 1844 received a patent for a so-called rotary rocket. He produced several designs, including one with curved vanes that were acted on by the motor efflux and another with angled nozzles to induce the desired spin. In addition to being more accurate, Hale's rocket eliminated the need for Congreve's guiding stick. It quickly replaced the Congreve rocket in military service.

Russian rocketry and the first MRLs

In Europe, 16 nations had rocket programs during the 19th century. Russia was a pioneer of modern rocketry and fielded its first military rocket in 1817. A rocket company was added to the establishment of the Russian army in 1827 and rockets were extensively used during the Russo-Turkish war of 1828–1829. The Russians also fielded a towed 6-round MRL in that conflict. Rocket development continued steadily and the Russians even developed and tested a rocket-firing submarine in 1834.

In the second half of the 1800s, the proliferation of rifling, breechloading, and advances in metallurgy increased the capability of conventional guns and they soon eclipsed rockets in importance as an artillery weapon.

Rocketry underwent a renaissance in the 1920s and 1930s. In the Soviet Union, the Gas Dynamics Laboratory (GDL) was formed at the end of the 1920s and concentrated on the research and development of solid fuel rockets. A separate organization, the Group for the Study of Jet Propulsion

The KARST-1 (Short Rocket Artillery System for Tanks-1) mounted on a KV-1. It consisted of four boxes each containing two M-13 rockets on the tank's fenders. The fixed launchers had to be aimed by steering the tank and the driver had a firing device and inclinometer. The low elevation of the launchers limited the range of the rockets to 600–800m. It did not enter production. (Author)

The first ZiS-6-based prototype with transverse-mounted launcher. (M. Foedrowitz)

> **MRL-ASSOCIATED TERMS**
> **BM** (Boyevaya Mashina) – Combat Vehicle. A launch vehicle consists of a launcher assembly mounted on a wheeled or tracked chassis.
> **Kompleks** (Complex) – The Complex includes the launch vehicle, a dedicated resupply transporter/reloader, rockets, associated tools and training devices, and fire control, survey and meteorological vehicles.
> **RSZO** (Reaktivnaya Sistema Zalpovogo Ognya) – Rocket system for salvo fire, a generic term for MRLs.
> **TZM** (Transportno-Zaryazhayushchaya Mashina) – Transporter-Reloading Vehicle. A vehicle used to resupply MRLs with rockets, often referred to as a transloader.

(GIRD) was later established that focused on liquid propellant systems. The GDL and the Moscow-based arm of the GIRD were merged into the Jet Propulsion Scientific Research Institute (RNII) in 1933.

The introduction of new solid fuel propellants gave impetus to a number of improved Russian military rockets and launch platforms. Among these and most relevant to the history of Soviet and Russian multiple rocket launchers were the fin-stabilized RS-82 82mm and RS-132 132mm air-to-ground rockets.

Development of ground-based MRLs by the RNII can be documented as early as 1936. In 1938, one of the projects undertaken by Scientific

The first production model of the BM-13. (Peter Kravchuk)

UNDERSTANDING MRL DESIGNATORS

One of the functions of Russia's Main Artillery Directorate (GAU) was the creation of a designation system for artillery weapons. In World War II, self-propelled ground MRLs received a designator with the "BM" prefix followed by a one- or two-digit suffix that identified the diameter of the rocket in centimeters (The BM-31 was an exception, as it fired a 300mm rocket). Variations of the basic launch vehicle that were capable of carrying a different number of rockets on the launcher received an additional numerical suffix indicating the quantity of rockets.

The launchers themselves, whether on a non-self-propelled mount or other ground vehicle – such as an armored train – followed the same pattern except they had an "M" prefix.

MRLs used by the Russian navy used a slightly different system. The mounts originally used for naval purposes were adapted from ground vehicles and received the designators M-x-M (M – Morskoy = sea) where the middle digit was the diameter of the rocket in centimeters. Later purpose-built naval mounts followed a different scheme, similar to the basic launcher designation except with the number of rockets listed first (e.g. 16-M-13).

The pattern for self-propelled launchers lasted into the early postwar period as the GAU was reorganized into the Main Rocket and Artillery Directorate (GRAU). It was later discontinued in favor of the GRAU industrial designators, although many writers in the West simply continued to apply the BM-xx designators. For example, the 220-mm 9P140 Uragan was referred to first as the BM-27 and then as the BM-22, despite the fact that it had only officially been assigned the 9P140 GRAU industrial designator.

The GRAU industrial designator follows a digit-letter-digit(s) format. The first digit identifies the category of equipment (9 = rockets), the letter is the role of the equipment (P initially, A subsequently = launcher; K = complex; M = rocket; N = warhead or submunition; T = transloader/resupply vehicle; V = command and control), and the remaining digits were the series and unique project identifiers.

Minor changes to a system not affecting its combat capabilities were assigned a numerical suffix (e.g. 9A52-2); more significant changes resulted in the addition of the suffix "M," and major changes in combat capability resulted in the assignment of a new project identifier. A specialized variant of the launcher would also be assigned a letter suffix depending on the role (e.g. BM-21V – Vozdushnodesantiy = airborne).

Cover names were also established, with violent weather phenomena being assigned to MRLs.

Research Institute-3 (NII-3) – the successor organization to the RNII – was a truck-mounted launcher for 132mm M-13 rockets. Derived from the RS-132, the M-13 rocket had a longer range (just under 8.5km), a better aerodynamic shape, and a larger warhead with almost 5kg of explosive. The fin-stabilized rocket was simple to produce, but relatively inaccurate.

The first prototype of the system was the MU-1 (Mechanized Installation – 1st Pattern). Based on the 4 x 2 ZiS-5 chassis, it had a transverse-mounted launcher with 24 aircraft-type launching rails. Testing revealed a number of serious issues, including stability problems caused by firing rockets to the side that further reduced the rocket's accuracy; an inconvenient and slow reloading process that resulted from the use of the front-loading aircraft rails; damage to the launch vehicle caused by the rocket's exhaust; and the poor cross-country mobility of the ZiS-5 chassis. In 1939, two more prototypes followed using the three-axle ZiS-6 chassis that had somewhat better cross-country performance. The first ZiS-6-based prototype also used a transverse-mounted launcher, but with traverse and elevation mechanisms and a slightly different arrangement of launching rails.

The second prototype, the MU-2, had the launcher mounted parallel to the long axis of the truck that, in combination with the use of jacks, made for a much more stable launch platform. In addition, a longer and redesigned type of launch rail further improved accuracy and enabled the launch rail to be loaded from the back, which made reloading easier. Each rail carried two rockets, one on top of the rail and the other below. The launcher had simple traverse and elevation controls, a conventional artillery sight mounted on the left of the

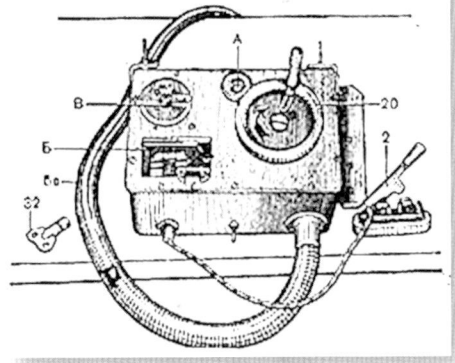

The simple firing device in the BM-13's cab consisted of a key-activated on-off switch, indicator window, fuses, knife switch, and handwheel. The operator's manual directed the gunner to close the knife switch, insert the key and turn it to the "on" position and rotate the handwheel for 17 full revolutions at the speed of two revolutions per second. Turning the handwheel completed the circuitry that launched the rockets. It would have been familiar to BM-21 gunners of today, as the early models of the BM-21 employ a similar device. (Author)

launcher, and a firing device mounted inside the cab. Armored shutters protected the cab windows. This established the basic configuration that almost all subsequent Russian and Soviet MRLs would follow. It was renamed the BM-13.

WORLD WAR II MRLs

BM-13

In addition to further minor improvements to the BM-13, the 1940 to early 1941 period saw work on tank, sled, and trailer-mounted launchers using a variety of rocket sizes. Immediately prior to their involvement in World War II, the Soviets decided to focus on the production of the BM-13. Production began at the Comintern plant in Voronezh, followed by a number of others including the Compressor plant in Moscow, which would become the factory most closely associated with MRL production.

A tracked version of the launcher was fielded in the fall of 1941 on the robust but slow STZ-5 tractor to improve mobility of the launcher and compensate for shortages of the ZiS-6 truck. One of the features was that it was capable of a zero degree elevation that permitted it to be used in a direct fire role.

As the Soviets began to receive western trucks through the Lend-Lease program, the launcher was standardized to enable it to be mounted on any truck chassis. A number of truck models were used as the chassis for MRLs including Chevrolet, GMC, International, Fordson, and Ford Marmon-Herrington, with the Studebaker US6 being the one most commonly used. In 1943, the standardized system was designated the BM-13N (Normalizovannaya = Normalized).

The payload, range, and accuracy of the M-13 were still problematic. To address these issues, the Soviets fielded three new rockets.

The M-20 was longer (2,090mm vs. 1,415mm) than the M-13 and had a larger warhead at the cost of a reduced range of 5km. Its heavier weight meant it could only be safely fired from the top of the launch rails, effectively cutting in half the number of rockets that could be fired in a single salvo. Moreover, their fragmentation effect was less than anticipated and production ended in mid-1944 after only two years.

Another long-range 132mm rocket, the M-13DD, entered service in late 1944. It had two stacked M-13 motor sections joined by an intermediate connector that burned simultaneously, giving it a range of 11.8km. As with the M-20, the increased weight meant that only the top of the launch rails

LEFT: A BM-13 using the STZ-5 chassis. Production of this model was ended as modern western trucks arrived in the Soviet Union. (Strategia KM Archive)

RIGHT: The BM-13N. Fifty-four percent of all BM-13s were based on the Studebaker US6 chassis. Here a column of BM-13Ns passes T-34s near Stalingrad in the winter of 1942. Note the crewmembers riding on the outside of the vehicle behind the cab, a very uncomfortable arrangement in bad weather. External seating for a portion of the crew was found on all of the wartime and some of the postwar truck-based MRLs. As can be seen in this photograph, a canvas cover could be fitted over the launcher when traveling for protection from the elements. (Peter Kravchuk)

could be used. Propellant gases from the upper motor were vented through oblique holes. However, the rotational effect of the rocket damaged the launcher rails during firing, so it was restricted to being launched from the later BM-13SN.

LEFT BM-13Ns of the 3rd Ukrainian Front advance in mid-1944. The number of MRLs increased dramatically as the war progressed. In the final years, they represented a large and important element of Soviet fire support. (Courtesy of the Central Museum of the Armed Forces, Moscow, via Stavka)

The M-13UK used a series of oblique vent holes at the top of the motor section to generate a stabilizing spin. The use of propellant gases for this purpose reduced the range to 7.9km but the gain in accuracy offset this and the rocket was adopted for service.

Spin could also be imparted via the launcher and designers at the Compressor plant introduced a new 10-rocket launch vehicle designated BM-13SN. The launcher consisted of four box-shaped frames holding spiral guide rods to spin the rockets as they were fired. This improved the accuracy of the rockets by the following magnitudes: M-13 missiles – 3.2; M-13UK – 1.1; M-20 – 3.3; M-13DD – 1.47. As can be seen, the rockets that lacked an inherent spin stabilization mechanism received a much greater benefit from this modification.

M-13 launchers were mounted on armored railway carriages for the defense of Moscow and subsequently formed part of the armored trains, numbers 686 and 697, of the 57th Separate Armored Train Battalion.

The M-13 also saw service afloat. The first models, the M-13-M1 and M-13-M2, were adaptations of the land-based launcher. The M-13-M1 had one set of eight rails capable of launching 16 rockets and the M-13-M2 had two sets of rails holding 32 rockets. The prototype was installed on a Project 1124 armored cutter and the mounting was adopted in late 1942. Experience of operating MRLs at sea revealed the need for improvements, such as a more reliable device for locking the rockets to the launch rails, so an improved through-deck mount – the 16-M-13 – entered service in 1945. A total of 65 M-13-M series and 16-M-13 launchers were delivered to the navy.

The 16-M-13 replaced the aft turret on some Project 1124 armored cutters and was employed against targets both on shore and at sea. (Ivan Chernikov)

LEFT: Crews load their BM-13Ns prior to a fire mission in the summer of 1943. The rockets came packed in crates of two. The method of manual loading changed little through the years and, even today, photos can be found showing BM-21 crewmen in virtually identical poses. (Strategia KM Archive)

RIGHT: The BM-13SN. About 100 BM-13SNs were produced in 1945 and apparently saw service until the early 1950s. (S. Gurov)

The origin of the BM-13's nickname "Katyusha" is lost to history, but there are a number of theories. Of these, perhaps the most compelling is that it was borrowed from a song of the same name that was popular at the time. The name was also used generically for other MRLs, being also applied to the BM-8 and sometimes to the BM-31 as well.

BM-8

Development of the BM-8 began shortly after that of the BM-13. It fired the 82mm M-8, a modified version of the RS-82 air-to-ground rocket. There were several variants of the M-8 rocket, the latest of which had a range of 5.5km and a warhead with .69kg of explosive. While the rocket had a short range and small warhead, it was adequate for the intended task of attacking infantry and crew-served weapons in the open or in lightly constructed field fortifications. The small size and light weight of the rockets permitted the development of small, man-portable, eight-round launchers and vehicle-mounted systems capable of firing up to 48 rockets without reloading.

A — BM-13N, BM-13 ON STZ-5, AND BM-31-12

1: The BM-13N became the standard model of the BM-13 family. It used the chassis of the Studebaker US6, a 6 x 6 2.5-ton truck designed for off-road use and exported to the Soviet Union in large numbers. By the end of World War II, over half of the BM-13s produced were of this model. Remounted on more modern truck chassis, they had a long service life in the postwar Soviet Army.

2: As with the BM-8-24, the Soviets turned to a tracked platform to overcome the mobility limitations imposed by the BM-13's ZiS-6 chassis. The STZ-5 tractor chosen had good cross-county mobility, but was slow and had a short cruising range. It was a stopgap measure that was abandoned as soon as modern trucks with good off-road performance became available from the West.

3: The BM-31-12 can be easily distinguished from other truck-based MRLs by its frame-type launcher, the only one of its type in World War II. Like the BM-13N and BM-8-48, it used the Studebaker US6 chassis, underscoring the importance of this vehicle. Although not a glamorous piece of equipment, the Studebaker US6 played a vital role in the mechanization of the Soviet military and helped make possible its dramatic advances in the final months of the war.

The BM-8-48 on a Chevrolet G-7171 chassis in the summer of 1944. (M. Morozow/M. Kolomiets)

The M-8-24 mount on the armored train *Kozma Minin*. (Strategia KM Archive)

The ability to fire large numbers of rockets from a single launcher produced a more even distribution of destructive effects than its 132mm counterparts.

NII-3 and the Compressor factory carried out design work in mid-1941. Two prototypes, each having 38 launch rails similar to those used on aircraft, were constructed on the ZiS-5 and ZiS-6 truck chassis. The number of launch rails was subsequently reduced to 36 in order to improve safety, and the system was adopted for serial production as the BM-8. Some appeared on the GAZ-AAA truck chassis due to shortages of the ZiS-6.

The BM-8 on the ZiS-6 chassis suffered from the same mobility problems as the BM-13. In addition, the short range of the M-8 rocket forced the BM-8 to approach relatively close to enemy lines, increasing its vulnerability to enemy fire. Accordingly, development and trials of a tracked variant based on the T-40 and T-60 light tank and capable of launching 24 rockets were conducted in September and October 1941. The aircraft-type launch rails were replaced by new ones similar to those on the BM-13 that were more suitable for a ground vehicle and that possessed an improved ignition system for the rockets. The trials revealed a significant increase in mobility and the ability to employ the rockets in a direct fire role, while the new launch rails improved both firing accuracy and reliability. The system was adopted as the BM-8-24 and 50 to 60 were produced. They were in service until the spring of 1943.

In 1942, a new launcher for 48 rockets was constructed using two sets of launch rails of the type used on the BM-8-24. This new launch vehicle, designated BM-8-48, used a variety of chassis and became the standard version used until the end of the war. Rockets could be fired in groups of three or a full volley of 48.

Perhaps as a way of economizing on the use of their imported trucks, the Soviets added a third set of 12 launch rails to create the BM-8-72. They appeared in the postwar victory parade, but there is no record of their use in combat.

A number of other platforms were used as the basis for 82mm MRLs. As the M-8 rocket was relatively small and light, a man-portable MRL was fielded in 1942 for use in difficult terrain where larger artillery weapons were impractical. The "mountain Katyusha" was mounted on a four-legged stand that could be disassembled into three parts for transport and on the wheeled Sokolov mount normally used for the Maxim machine gun. It saw service in the Caucasus Mountains and in Crimea. Another lightweight version was the BM-8-8, which was mounted on jeeps provided under the Lend-Lease program. Fielded in 1944, it was used in the Carpathian Mountains.

The 82mm MRLs also formed part of the armament of armored trains. Two 48-round launchers were mounted on armored railway wagons and took part, along with their 132mm analogs, in the battle for Moscow. In addition, the armored trains *Kozma Minin* and *Ilya Muromets* had railway wagons armed with the M-8-24.

M-30

The Soviet's first indigenous heavy MRL was the M-30 launcher, deployed in June 1942 in an attempt to achieve greater target effects than possible with the M-13 rocket. Like the German schweres Wurfgerät 41, the M-30 launcher was a simple inclined metal frame that could be adjusted for elevation and had an electric firing device. The frame held four M-30 fin-stabilized 300mm rockets that were transported in and fired from special wooden crates, similar to their 28cm and 32cm German analogs. The M-30 launcher could also be fitted with six rails for M-20 rockets.

The M-30 launcher could be produced quickly and inexpensively and was easy to load. The design, however, had a number of important disadvantages. It lacked mobility, changes in traverse required the shifting of the entire frame, and the process of positioning the frames, loading them, and making the necessary electrical firing connections was very slow. The short range of the rockets, only 2,800m, which required these activities to be carried out in close proximity to the enemy, compounded these disadvantages. Moreover, the short packing/firing crates provided poor directional control for the rockets that, unlike their German counterparts,

The M-28

The surrounded defenders of Leningrad produced an improvised copy of the German 280mm rocket, its box-type transport and launch container, and inclined launching frame in May 1942. The launching frame was made of wood or metal and supported two and four rockets, respectively. The M-28 had a maximum range of 3,000m. It saw limited combat service during the siege. For example, 392 M-28 rockets were used to disrupt a planned German assault on 20 June. They were organized into battalions of three batteries. Each battery had three platoons of 16 M-28s each.

were not spin stabilized. As a result of this and the poor aerodynamic shape of the rockets, accuracy was poor, even by MRL standards.

To address the issue of the M-30 rocket's short range, the M-31 rocket was introduced in late 1942. This new rocket was longer and had a range of 4,325m. The M-30 launcher could be used to fire M-31 rockets, but was supplanted by a new M-31 launcher that was shortly followed by a modified version capable of firing eight rockets mounted in two tiers of four. A trailer-mounted version later underwent trials but was not adopted.

BM-31-12

As World War II entered a more mobile phase and the mobility limitations of the M-30 launcher became increasingly apparent, work began on a truck-mounted system, the BM-31-12, which was adopted for service in mid-1944. The most distinctive visual feature of the new launcher was the use of a welded metal frame containing 12 individual cells instead of the launch rails used on earlier MRLs. It incorporated a new electrical ignition system and locking mechanisms to support more securely the front and rear of the projectile in transit and prevent accidental ignition. This enabled the launcher frame to be loaded in a secure area and driven to the firing site.

The BM-31-12 used the chassis of the Studebaker US6 truck and after the war would serve for another decade mounted on a ZiS-151 chassis.

Projectile	M-8	M-13	M-13	M-13UK	M-13DD	M-20	M-28	M-30	M-31	M-31UK
Adoption Date	1944	1941	1942	1944	1944	1942	1942	1942	1943	1944
Caliber (mm)	82	132	132	132	132	132	280	300	300	300
Explosive Weight (kg)	0.6	4.9	4.9	4.9	4.9	18.4	45.4	28.9	28.9	28.9
Maximum Range (m)	5,515	8,470	8,230	7,900	11,800	5,000	1,900	2,800	4,325	4,000
Dispersion at Max Range – Deflection/ Range (m)	105/220	135/300	100/155	84/107	120/179	85/111	47.5/38	90/140	105/255	55/75

B   BM-8-36, BM-8-24 AND BK-1125 ARMORED GUNBOAT

1: The BM-8-36 used aircraft-type launching rails, much like the first BM-13 prototypes. While their use leveraged existing production of this type of rail and perhaps shortened development time of the system, their short length provided little directional guidance to the rockets. BM-8-36s were produced at the Compressor and Krasnaya Presnya factories.

2: The short range of the 82mm rockets meant the unarmored BM-8-36 had to be located close to the front lines, increasing its risk of being hit by enemy fire. Moreover, the 6 x 4 ZiS-6 truck had poor off-road mobility. The solution to these issues was the BM-8-24, mounted on a chassis of the T-40 and, later, the T-60 light tanks (as shown here), which had rapidly diminishing value as armored fighting vehicles. Firing could be accomplished under armor and the tracked chassis provided greater mobility. In addition, the new, longer type of launch rails provided better directional control for the rockets, improving their accuracy.

3: The BK-1125 class of small armored cutters had a number of different armament configurations; one had a 24-M-8 launcher mounted aft, as shown here. The small size of the 82mm M-8-M and 24-M-8 launchers meant that they could be mounted on a variety of smaller craft, including the G-5 and Ya-5 torpedo boats. They performed useful service as part of the various river flotillas, where they provided fire support to the ground forces.

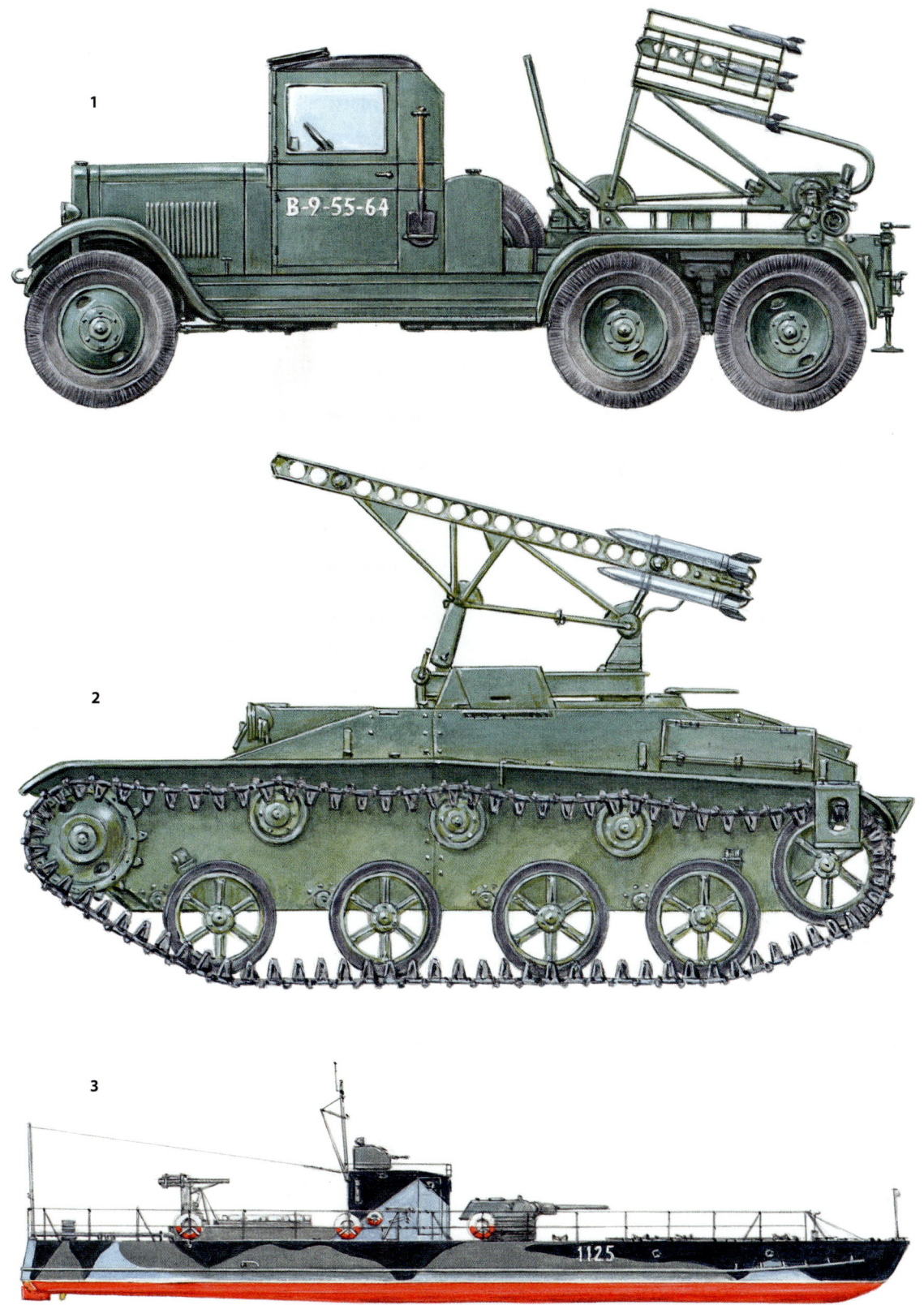

A loaded BM-31-12 in Berlin sits ready to fire with the armored shields protecting the cab and the stabilizing jacks at the rear of the chassis in the lowered position. About 1,800 BM-31-12s were fielded during the war. It was first used in combat on July 17, 1944 near the village of Nalyuchi. As with the BM-13, the BM-31-12 acquired a nickname. The official nickname was "Andryusha," but it was much more widely known by soldiers as "Luka," from the name of the central character in a bawdy poem. (State Archive of Ukraine)

Concurrently, the M-31UK rocket was introduced to address the relatively poor accuracy of the M-30 and M-31. This rocket differed from the M-31 largely in that four metal tubes extended perpendicular from the rocket's body, just behind the warhead. A hole near the end of each tube vented propellant gases, causing the rocket to spin. The stabilizing effect reduced the dispersion of the warheads at the cost of a slight decrease in range to 4,000m.

Organization

The organization of Soviet MRLs evolved continually over the course of World War II, but is too complex to recount in detail here. The following provides an overview of MRL organizational changes.

The first ten rocket artillery units were independent batteries. At this early stage the numbers of launchers in the battery was fluid, typically varying from between four and nine, with four later becoming the standard battery complement. In several cases, the batteries went into action under strength with as few as three launchers. Nine of the batteries were equipped exclusively with BM-13s and the other with two BM-13s and two BM-8-36s. A single 122mm M-10/30 howitzer was also included in the battery for registration purposes. (The 122mm howitzer was later found to be useless for registration and was dropped from the battery's equipment authorization.) These independent batteries were later absorbed into larger MRL units.

In practice, it was found that a higher density of fire than a battery-sized unit could produce was needed and accordingly, in early August 1941, the first eight Guards Mortar Regiments were formed as part of the RVGK (Reserve of the Supreme Command). Designation as an RVGK asset allowed these units to be used on the most critical areas of the front, especially in support of breakthrough operations requiring a high density of artillery support. These regiments had a triangular structure of three MRL battalions composed of three batteries with four BM-8s or BM-13s each, for a total of 36 launchers.

The wide demand for MRL support quickly led the Soviets to field individual battalions, usually in support of infantry divisions. In addition, nine of the first 14 MRL regiments were reorganized into 28 separate Guards

A battery of BM-8-36s in action in 1942. Almost 350 were fielded before it was supplanted by the BM-8-48. (Strategia KM Archive)

mortar battalions. There were two different structures for these separate battalions, one with three batteries and one with two batteries. Each battery had eight BM-8s or BM-13s.

The regiments were reorganized in early 1942. The three battalions were reduced from three to two batteries each and the batteries reduced to four launchers for a total of 24 launchers in the regiment.

As the M-30 was fielded in 1942, it was organized into battalions of three batteries. Each M-30 battery had 32 launching frames. An M-30 battalion with 96 launching frames quickly proved difficult to resupply, and the number of batteries was reduced to two and the total number of launching frames was halved, to 48.

At the end of 1942, another major reorganization took place to support the transition to offensive operations. This involved the formation of MRL brigades and divisions. The M-30 brigades consisted of five 48-launching frame battalions. The divisions were composite units with two M-30 brigades and four BM-13 regiments. The M-30 brigades lacked an adequate number of ammunition resupply trucks and, as can easily be imagined, the composite divisions equipped with both the highly mobile BM-13s and almost static M-30 launching frames proved awkward to employ.

Both units were quickly replaced with new structures. The M-30 brigades were reduced to four battalions, but each battalion was increased in size from two to three batteries. The brigade now had 288 M-30s rather than the 240 under the previous organization, but the organic transport was significantly increased to address the ammunition resupply issue. In the divisions, the BM-13s were replaced by a third M-30 brigade.

The introduction of the heavy BM-31 into service in 1944 resulted in a new brigade organization for it. Structurally, it resembled the first BM-8/BM-13 regiment, having three battalions each with three subordinate batteries and four BM-31s per battery.

M-31 launchers in action. Although time-consuming to emplace, the large warheads were very effective, even against bunkers and other reinforced field fortifications. The 7th Guards Mortar Division, equipped with 432 of the similar M-30 launchers, fired two salvos at the beginning of the Smolensk offensive, destroying 550m of trenchline, 114 lightly constructed dugouts, 27 bunkers and 66 guns and mortars. The warheads of both the M-30 and M-31 rockets contained 28.9kg of explosive and were capable of creating a crater with a diameter of 7–8m and a depth of 2–2.5m. It could also penetrate a brick wall 75cm thick. (M. Foedrowitz)

Production

The Soviet resource commitment to fielding of MRLs during the war was enormous. By the time the war ended, the Soviet army boasted 40 separate battalions (38 equipped with BM-13s and two with BM-8s), 115 regiments (96 BM-13s and 19 BM-8s), 22 separate brigades (9 M-31s and 13 BM-31-12s) and seven divisions. Over 10,000 BM-8s, BM-13s and BM-31-12s were produced along with more than 12.5 million rockets, of which 7.5 million were expended in combat.

The rapid growth in the number of MRLs as well as their demonstrated value in operations translated into a corresponding increase in the density of these systems at the front. This increase was particularly dramatic at the end of the war as MRLs were massed to support the final offensive operations. In 1944 there were an average of 8–12 MRLs for each kilometer of front for breakthrough operations; by the beginning of 1945 this had grown to 15–20. Almost 60 percent of the BM-8 and BM-13 regiments and more than 75 percent of the BM-31-12 units supported the 2nd and 3rd Belorussian and 1st Baltic fronts in the East Prussian offensive and the 1st and 2nd Byelorussian and 1st Ukrainian fronts in the final assault against Berlin.

OPERATIONAL USE

The primary targets for MRLs have remained largely unchanged since the introduction of the BM-13: troops in the open or in light field fortifications, and concentration areas for men and materiel. The introduction of larger and longer-range rockets and new warheads expanded and improved the effectiveness of MRL missions, but didn't fundamentally change their nature. For example, heavier warheads made attacks against deeper field fortifications and buildings a practical option. Tanks, which had always been vulnerable to all but the smallest rockets, can now be more effectively attacked with specialized anti-armor submunitions.

Tactics have also remained relatively static, driven in part by the large signature of the rocket exhaust plumes and the almost universal use of unarmored transport vehicles. Loaded MRLs would take up their positions, fire, and quickly withdraw. Only in the most benign combat environments

C — ORSHA – BM-13's COMBAT DEBUT.

The first Soviet multiple rocket launcher unit was formed on June 28, 1941 under the command of Captain Ivan Flerov. The combat elements of this experimental unit consisted of a single battery of seven BM-13s and a 122mm M1910/1930 towed howitzer used for registration purposes. Reflecting the dire military situation, crews received only four days' training – an achievement made possible by the BM-13's extreme simplicity – and operational testing would be conducted in combat.

Setting off from Moscow for the front by road, the battery arrived in its operational area two days later and was attached to the 20th Army. Its first missions were against targets in Orsha. Located at the confluence of the Dnieper and Orshitsa rivers, Orsha was a river port and a vital rail junction. The first action, as recorded in the unit's wartime diary, is depicted here. Just after 3pm on July 14, the battery launched its rockets against the German trains at the Orsha railway junction and station. The attack caused great devastation and the diary records the target area as being "a sea of fire." Later that same afternoon, the battery conducted a second attack, this time against a concentration of German forces waiting to cross the Orshitsa River. The concentration consisted of convoys of tanks and other armor, transport vehicles including horse carts, and infantry units. One of the battery's forward observers recorded the effects of the strike, noting the great loss of enemy materiel and personnel and the panic that gripped the survivors.

Over the next three months, the battery took part in a number of other actions. Meanwhile, other independent BM-13 batteries were fielded as well; following the fielding of the tenth such unit in September, they were absorbed into larger units. As at Orsha, these caused not only heavy losses, but had a devastating effect on morale. Soviet after-action reports and the interrogation of German prisoners indicated that the effect of the strikes crushed German resistance. The sudden and overwhelming volume of firepower often caused the survivors to flee and sometimes caused units adjacent to the target area to do so as well. Captain Flerov's battery, along with other Soviet units, was caught in an encirclement at the beginning of October. Attempting to break out and short on fuel, Flerov was forced to destroy most of his transport. He was killed in an ambush that eliminated his remaining vehicles. A monument at Orsha commemorates his battery's historic attack.

A crew from the Dnieper River Flotilla ties up their boat equipped with a 24-M-8. Standardized naval mounts for 82mm rockets were also developed following testing of improvised mounts. The M-8-M was adapted from a land mount and used on the Project 1125 armored cutters and several types of torpedo boats. There was also an 8-rocket 8-M-8 launcher and the later, improved through-deck mount was the 24-M-8. One hundred and forty one of both the M-8-M and 24-M-8 mounts were produced. (Strategia KM Archive)

would these valuable assets fire repeated salvos from the same position.

The initial combat actions of the first Soviet independent MRL batteries were typical of the missions assigned to MRLs. Captain Ivan Flerov's battery was first used against enemy concentrations (see previous page), one a logistics installation and the other a large group of forces that had assembled at a river crossing site. Lieutenant Alexander Kun's battery was placed under the control of the 19th Army. Its earliest missions included strikes on tanks and infantry in an assembly area as they prepared to attack. Lieutenant Nikolai Denisenko's small battery of three BM-13s conducted an attack to destroy an enemy defensive position near Yartsev while under the control of Lieutenant General Konstantin Rokossovsky, who judged the strike as highly successful. On August 6, 1941, a battery of four BM-13s under the command of Senior Lieutenant Denisov fired three salvos in support of a counterattack by the 53rd Rifle Division/43rd Army. This reportedly enabled the division to seize the enemy strong points in its sector with very few casualties.

As already noted, given the limited number of MRL units available and the heavy defensive fighting resulting from German offensive operations in mid- to late-1941, the Soviets had little option but to temporarily suspend plans to form regiment-sized MRL units. Instead, they fielded independent battalions and parceled them out to support divisions defending the most critical sectors. As this occurred, so apparently did instances of the inappropriate employment of MRLs by senior commanders.

In order to correct this, the Stavka felt compelled to issue Directive 002490, *Commander of fronts and armies on the use of rocket launchers* on October 1, 1941. The Directive read, in part:

> Units of the Red Army recently received a powerful new weapon in the form of M-8 and M-13 combat vehicles, the best means to destroy (neutralize) enemy personnel, its tanks, motorized units, and weapons.
> Sudden, massive and accurate fire from M-8 and M-13 battalions provides exceptionally good results against the enemy and at the same time has a strong moral shock on its manpower, resulting in a loss of combat capability. This is particularly true at the moment when the enemy infantry has more tanks than we do and when our infantry are most in need of strong support from the M-8 and M-13, which are capable of being successfully used against tanks.
> Due to the fact that BM-8 and BM-13 are underestimated by our officers and often used completely incorrectly, the Supreme Command orders:
> – M-8 and M-13 battalions and batteries are to be used against large, reconnoitered targets (concentrations of infantry, motorized units, tanks, artillery, and crossing sites). Fire on individual small targets is strictly prohibited.
> – Depending on the situation, the M-8 and M-13 battery and battalions perform the following main tasks: a) during the offense, or during

counterattacks, when the enemy infantry rises up and the enemy tanks and motorized units leave their cover and are in the open, employ massive M-8 and M-13 fire on enemy manpower, tanks and motorized units; b) during the offense and our counterattacks employ massive M-8 and M-13 fire in order to break through the enemy defenses and to expand the breakthrough. Our infantry attack should be carried out simultaneously with the firing of the M-8 and M-13 batteries; c) if on the defensive bring the M-8 and M-13 fire on concentrations of enemy manpower, tanks and motorized units of the enemy; d) during any conditions employ M-8 and M-13 batteries against the enemy at crossings and narrow defiles; e) in all these cases, do not use individual M-8s and M-13s, but whole battalions. It is strictly forbidden to use M-8 and M-13 projectiles for ranging and strongly recommended to use regimental guns for this purpose.

As German forces advanced to the outskirts of Moscow in late 1941, the Soviets rushed MRL units to the defense of the capital. Reflecting the importance of defending the city, most of the Soviet's MRLs were concentrated there with the number of MRL battalions growing from 13 in late October to 36 by early December. They were rushed to where the threats were greatest and played a critical role in halting the German attacks. As the crisis passed and the Soviets launched their counteroffensive, the MRLs advanced as well and were used to soften the German defensive positions and repel counterattacks.

The strategic transition to a general offensive was facilitated by the consolidation of the independent battalions into regiments. This was done not only to address the command problems inherent in controlling a large number of battalions but to comply with the Stavka's requirement that artillery be massed to support attacks in the most important sectors. Offensive operations were also aided by development of the M-20 and M-30 rockets, which with their large warheads were better able to deal with German field fortifications.

At Stalingrad, the growth in the number of MRLs, and the formation of larger units, allowed them to play an even more vital role than they had at Moscow. Twenty-six regiments and one separate battalion were employed at Stalingrad by November 1942.

In their article *Creation and Development of Rocket Artillery in the First Phase of the War*, Lieutenant General of Artillery P. Degtyarev and Colonel V. Gurkin note that MRL units:

> ...participated in all phases of the defensive battle: they supported the fighting of the 62nd and 64th Armies' forward units on the far approaches to the city; they destroyed personnel and equipment where they were concentrating and also when they were on the move; they were active in repelling the massed

A fully loaded Egyptian BM-24 sits abandoned during the 1967 Six-Day War. This photo shows details of the launcher, including the electrical contacts at the rear of the launcher used to ignite the rockets. (Israel Defense Forces)

infantry and armored attacks on the defensive lines around Stalingrad; and they provided support for the counterattacks by our forces. For the first time rocket launchers were used in combat operations within a large city.

The role taken by rocket artillery in the defensive fighting for Stalingrad may be followed using the example of the combat actions of the 83rd Guards Mortar Regiment (commanded by Colonel K.T. Golubev). The regiment, which was equipped with BM-8 rocket launchers mounted on T-60 light tanks, went to Stalingrad as soon as it was formed and was assigned to the 62nd Army. Together with the troops of this famous army, the soldiers of the regiment went through the awesome defense of the hero city. Going into action on the far approaches to Stalingrad near Chernyshev, the regiment supported the fighting of the forward element of the 33rd Rifle Division, subsequently using the firepower of its battalions to cover the army's withdrawal across the Don and support a counterattack by units of the 1st Tank Army west of Kalach. During the defensive battles the regiment took part in repelling massed infantry and tank attacks on the city's outer and inner rings, often having to fire from open firing positions, and during the encirclement it was in heavy fighting around Peskovatka and Vertyachii. But the real trials for the regiment's soldiers came with the terrible fighting in the city, which even turned into hand-to-hand combat. Together with the glorious soldiers of the 62nd Army, the guardsmen of the 83rd Regiment often had to defeat enemy attacks in close-quarters fighting and move their equipment to safe positions while under rifle and machine-gun fire … The regiment's battalions supported the combat actions of the glorious 13th and 37th Guards Rifle Divisions and 284th and 308th Rifle Divisions in the center of the city near the railway station and main landing, defending the Red October, Barrikady and STZ Factories and fighting on the Mamaev Kurgan.

The role of MRLs in the final battle of Berlin in 1945 and in the 1994–95 fighting for Grozny in Chechnya are described in the commentary below.

Most recently, the ongoing conflict in Eastern Ukraine provides many examples of the employment of MRLs. One such attack on July 11, 2014 illustrates a typical scenario. In this case, the target was a troop

D BATTLE OF BERLIN, APRIL 1945

By the time of the final assault on Berlin, multiple rocket launchers were a well-established and important component of Soviet fire support. Almost 375,000 82mm, 132mm and 300mm rockets were fired in the operation to take the city. In this scene – based on a period photograph – a crew reloads its BM-31-12. In the distance is another launcher from the same battery.

The nature of the terrain in urban operations makes target acquisition and adjusting fire difficult; tall buildings create large dead spaces that particularly affect low-angle fire, and friendly and enemy forces are often too close together for indirect fire to be used. On the other hand, the large high-explosive warheads typically found on MRL rockets were particularly useful against structures. Moreover, the Soviets overcame many of the limitations imposed by the terrain by frequently employing artillery – both cannon and rocket – in a direct fire role.

The next time Soviet MRLs would be extensively used in urban combat was during the 1990s in Grozny, the capital of Chechnya. In the 1994–1995 battle for the city, the Soviets largely limited the use of artillery due to collateral damage concerns. The Soviets' poor combat performance against a determined Chechen resistance led to a number of changes being implemented when the city had to be retaken in 1999–2000. Among these was the extensive use of artillery, including heavy MRLs such as the TOS-1. Although the Soviets were successful, the city was devastated and left in a state reminiscent of Berlin in 1945.

concentration area, specifically a bivouac area for a small element of a Ukrainian motorized rifle brigade near the town of Zelenopillya, about 9km from the Ukraine–Russia border. The attack by BM-21s took place in the early morning and killed 19 and wounded 93. In addition, numerous trucks and armored personnel carriers and at least one tank were destroyed in the attack.

COLD WAR AND MODERN MRLs

The Soviet experience in World War II established the MRL as an important component of the artillery. A 1946 study recommended the retention of the Studebaker US6-mounted BM-8-48, BM-13N and BM-31-12 in the active force structure and the Chevrolet-mounted BM-8-48 in the reserves. The BM-13Ns soldiered on for several more decades, first in an operational role and then as a training vehicle. They were also exported to Soviet client states such as Afghanistan and Libya. BM-13Ns were first remounted on the ZiS/Zil-151, an early postwar vehicle that copied a number of features from the Studebaker US6. In addition to the ZiS/Zil-151, the launcher also appeared on the Zil-157 (BM-13NM) and Zil-131 (BM-13NMM) chassis.

Not surprisingly, orders followed in early 1947 for a series of new MRLs to replace the wartime systems and requirements were issued later for systems with a much greater range.

The immediate postwar period saw the further development of spin stabilization – either alone or in combination with the use of fins – to improve the accuracy of the rockets. Launch tubes, rather than rails or frames, also appeared for the first time. Their use was limited at first to firing finless spin-stabilized rockets, as the fixed fins used by rockets during the early postwar period required a frame-type launcher. Folding fins would follow in later years, permitting what would become the standard arrangement of fin- and spin-stabilized rockets fired from launch tubes.

As in World War II, several of these new MRLs would also appear with specialized mounts on naval vessels.

BM-24

The BM-24 was the Soviet Union's first postwar MRL – entering service in 1951 – and was the replacement for the BM-31-12. It consisted of a launching frame for 12 240mm rockets mounted on a ZiS (later ZiL)-151 truck chassis. A later version of the BM-24 using the chassis of the ZiL-157 truck, a new gunner's sight, and incorporating other minor modifications was designated BM-24M.

Development of a tracked version of the BM-24 began as the wheeled version entered into service. Designated the BM-24T and fielded in 1956, it

Soviet crews reload their BM-24s. In the foreground, can be seen the loading tray which is attached to the launching frame. The heavy rocket is pushed into the frame with the aid of a ramrod, a necessary tool given the height of the launcher. (Author)

was based on the AT-S medium artillery tractor and was intended for use in armored formations. The launcher consisted of an array of tubes rather than the open frames used on the BM-24. They were shorter than the open frames but enabled the rockets to achieve the same ballistic performance.

The finless 240mm rockets were spin stabilized by the use of angled nozzles at the end of the rocket body. Five rocket types were available, three with high explosive warheads and two with warheads filled with the non-persistent nerve agent R-35 (Sarin). As can be seen in the table below, the MS-24UD rocket achieved its long range by reducing the warhead weight in favor of additional propellant.

Designation	Warhead Type	Warhead Weight (kg)	Propellant Weight (kg)	Length (mm)	Maximum Range (m)
M-24F	HE	60.8	16.2	1,124	6,575
M-24FUD	HE	46.5	23.9	1,245	10,600
MD-24F	HE	48.4	44.3	1,684	17,500
MS-24	Chemical	44.3	16.2	1,240	6,500
MS-24UD	Chemical	44.3	44.3	1,240	16,000

The standard M-24F rocket would typically produce a crater 5–6m in diameter and 3–4m deep.

The BM-24 was exported to several Warsaw Pact nations, Egypt, Syria, North Korea, Cuba and a number of Soviet client states in Africa. It was a long-lived weapon and saw service in the Soviet Union until the mid-1980s.

Israel improved BM-24s captured during the Six-Day War of 1967 by remounting them on ZiL-157s, adding a domestic new fire control system, and making several other minor modifications. A battalion of these BM-24s saw action on both the Syrian and Egyptian fronts in 1973 and again in Lebanon in 1982.

BM-14 and RPU-14

Developed concurrently with the BM-24, the BM-14 was the replacement for the BM-13 and was adopted in 1952 as the Soviet's division-level MRL.

Shown here are BM-14Ms. The BM-14 was widely exported to Soviet client states and enjoyed a long service life in countries that didn't require a heavier or more sophisticated MRL. (US Department of Defense)

LEFT: The RPU-14 was the only MRL available to the airborne troops until the introduction of the BM-21V. The box on the right of the launcher is the firing mechanism, with the cable leading to the remote firing device located up to 60m away. On the left of the launcher, not visible here, are the gunner's panoramic sight and traverse and elevation handwheels. (Author)

RIGHT: The A-22 Ogon, still being marketed today, was designed to be capable of firing M-14OF rockets, but that projectile has been supplanted by two types (high explosive and incendiary) of new rockets for the launcher. The Zubr-class air cushion landing craft shown here mounts two of the system's 22-round MS-227 retractable launchers. (Ministry of Defense – Russian Federation)

It followed the same configuration as the BM-24 and its World War II predecessors: a cargo truck with the cargo bed replaced by the launcher, fold-down metal shields that protected the glass portions of the cab during firing, seats for the crew behind the cab, stabilizing jacks at the rear of the chassis, and manual traverse and elevation controls. The launcher consisted of 16 relatively short tubes for 140mm rockets, arranged in two rows.

As with the BM-24, the BM-14 initially used the ZiS/Zil-151 chassis. However, as more capable truck chassis became available they replaced the older models and the modernized systems were given new designators: BM-14M for launch vehicles using the Zil-157 chassis and BM-14MM for those based on the Zil-131.

Another variant, the BM-14-17, was built on a 4 x 4 GAZ-63/63A chassis and had an additional launch tube for a total of 17 rockets. It provided a marginal increase in firepower and a 40-degree increase in traverse on a chassis that weighed a little more than half that of the ZiL-151/157. The BM-14-17 saw only limited Soviet and foreign service, as the BM-21, with its vastly increased firepower, was introduced just five years later. The system later appeared on a GAZ-66 chassis, and was designated the BM-14-17M.

Developed for use by airborne troops, the RPU-14 (Reaktivnaya Puskovaya Ustanovka = rocket launcher) consisted of an array of 16 short 140mm launching tubes mounted on the carriage of the D-44 85mm divisional gun. Small and lightweight, it was air-transportable and air-droppable. The RPU-14 was normally towed by the GAZ-66B, although it could be moved by any light vehicle or manhandled by its crew of five for short distances with the aid of a castor wheel on the carriage legs. It was exported to North Korea in small numbers.

The 140mm rockets fired by the BM-14 family of launchers were about the same size as the 132mm projectiles fired by the BM-13 and provided only a slight increase in range. The rockets, like those fired by the BM-24, were spin stabilized by angled nozzles in the base of the rocket rather than fins. There were three types of rockets available:

Designation	Warhead Type	Maximum Range (m)
M-14OF	HE	9,800
M-14D	Smoke	10,600
M-14	Chemical (Sarin)	9,800

The BMD-20 in travel configuration. The shutters used to protect the cab from the rocket exhaust are folded as are the stabilizing jacks at the rear of the chassis. The crew rides between the launcher and cab. Two of the spiral guide rails within the launcher frame are visible against the nearest rocket. (US Department of Defense)

The minimum range was normally about 7,500m, although a ring that acted as an air brake could be attached behind the fuse to reduce the range to 1,000m.

Although long out of service by today's Russian ground forces, BM-14-17s continue to serve in the naval sphere. The MAK-160 artillery ship has four 17-tube mounts amidships and the Shmel-class gunboat, an updated version of the armored cutters and other small craft that served in World War II, a single mount aft of the superstructure. The Soviet Polnochny-class landing ship mounted a pair of the very similar Polish WM-18 18-tube 140mm launchers.

BMD-20

Adopted for service at the same time as the BM-14, the BMD-20 consisted of a rectangular launching frame mounted on a ZiS/ZiL-151 truck. The frame contained spiral guide rails that supported four 200mm MD-20F rockets.

The MD-20F rockets were loaded manually with the assistance of a support tray and two tongs, a process that took about five minutes. The rocket had a maximum range of 18,750m and a 30kg high explosive warhead that formed a crater about 6m in diameter and 3m deep on impact. The fuse could be set for instantaneous or delayed action. The rockets were stabilized in flight by four fins and the spin induced by the spiral guide rails and angled nozzles at the end of the rocket body.

North Korea was the most prolific foreign user of the BMD-20, employing it in both ground and naval roles. A few were exported to Cuba and Ethiopia, where they were used in the Ogaden conflict with Somalia.

BM-25 Korshun (Kite)

The BM-25 responded to the need for a long-range bombardment system that could engage targets throughout the depth of enemy defenses. It consisted of a frame-type launcher holding six 250mm 3R7 rockets, each with a 100kg blast warhead, mounted on a YAZ(later KrAZ)-214 chassis. Unlike the solid propellant rockets typically used by other MRLs, the 3R7s used a storable liquid propellant consisting of kerosene (fuel) and nitric acid (oxidizer). This more energetic liquid propellant produced greater thrust and enabled the rockets to reach a range of 55km, far beyond that of other contemporary

Poor accuracy led to the end of BM-25 production after only three years. Also, the large rockets made it slow to reload, a process that took up to 20 minutes. (US Department of Defense)

MRLs or cannon artillery systems. Despite being both fin- and spin-stabilized, the rockets proved disappointingly inaccurate.

The BM-25 entered service in 1957, but because of the rocket's inaccuracy only a few launchers were fielded before production ended in 1960. Some were exported to South Yemen, where they saw their only combat use against North Yemen.

BM-21 Grad (Hail)

The BM-21 is the most numerous and widely deployed multiple rocket launcher in the world. More than 11,000 BM-21s and its variants have been produced and they have served in more than 50 countries. Despite their age, they remain the dominant MRL in use today. A simple and highly effective system, the launcher vehicles and rockets have been continually updated to incorporate emerging new technologies.

Development of the BM-21 began in 1960 in response to a GAU requirement. A partnership between the State Engineering Design Bureau located at the Compressor plant and NII-147 resulted in the 2B5 launch vehicle and a 122mm rocket with a high explosive warhead, the 9M21OF (later the redesignated 9M22U). The launcher was adopted as the BM-21 in 1963, part of the 9K51 complex.

The launch vehicle was mounted on the Ural-375D 6 x 6 truck, equipped with a centralized tire pressure regulation system for improved cross-country mobility. There were 40 launch tubes – rails and frames would no longer be used for Soviet or Russian MRLs – each of which had a spiral groove that engaged a lug on the rocket to impart a spin that helped stabilize the rocket in flight. Elevation and traverse of the

Evolution of 122mm Multiple Rocket Launchers

```
BM-21 ┬── 2B26
      ├── 9A51
      ├── BM-21V
      ├── BM-21-1 ── 2B17-1 (Tornado) ── 2B17M (Tornado G)
      ├── 9P138
      ├── 9P139
      └── BM-21PD
```

Note: Systems aligned vertically are of the same generation.

array was electric and there was a hydraulic locking mechanism for the launch tube array as well as one for the truck chassis that eliminated the need for stabilizing jacks. The array could be elevated from 0 to 55 degrees and traversed 102 degrees to the left and 70 degrees to the right. The firing of single rockets or salvos was possible, controlled by a firing device in the cab.

Rockets were normally delivered to the launcher by a suitable cargo truck in crates each containing one rocket. There was also a 9F37 rack that could be fitted in the bed of an ordinary cargo truck for transporting uncrated rockets. The resupply vehicle would later be standardized on a Ural-4320 chassis (the diesel-powered Ural-4320 is an improved version of the gasoline-powered Ural-375D) as the 9T254.

The designers abandoned the angled nozzles used by the BM-14 rockets for folding fins that were compatible with launch tubes. The spring-loaded fins deployed as soon as the rocket left the tube and had a small cant that helped maintain the spin generated by the tube's spiral groove. The groove widened at the back end of the tube to ease loading.

The number of available rocket types increased consistently over the years following the introduction of the basic 9M22U high explosive rocket and are shown below. The new rockets provided a greater variety of warheads and increased range.

LEFT: A battery of BM-21-1s firing. These vehicles have the thermal shield over the rear portion of the launch tubes, a feature not found on the earliest BM-21s. (Ministry of Defense – Russian Federation)

RIGHT: Although of indifferent quality, this remarkable image from a security camera video captures an MRL attack from the defender's perspective. In this case, Russian forces or their separatist proxies have fired a volley of 122mm rockets against a Ukrainian checkpoint near Volnovakha, 35km southwest of Donetsk. Most of the rockets have fallen short. However, one rocket flew long and landed approximately 12–15 meters from a civilian bus waiting to proceed through the checkpoint. Twelve people were killed, including nine women and a child, and another 17 were wounded. The conflict has been marked by Russian or separatist use of MRLs against civilians, including those in heavily populated urban areas. (Author)

Designation	Warhead Type	Warhead Weight (kg)	Maximum Range (km)
9M22U	HE	18.4	20.4 (12–16 with brake rings)
9M22S	Incendiary (180 submunitions)	N/A	N/A
9M28F	Separating HE fragmentation	21	15
9M28K	AT mine (Cluster – 3 PTM-3, 5kg magnetically activated mines)	22.8	13.4
9M42	Illumination	N/A	N/A
9M43	Smoke (5 submunitions)	20.2	20.2
9M53F	Separating HE fragmentation	26	20.5

Designation	Warhead Type	Warhead Weight (kg)	Maximum Range (km)
9M217	AT (Cluster – 2 sensor-fused submunitions)	25	30
9M218	AP/AT (Cluster – 45 dual-purpose submunitions)	25	30
9M519	Radio jammer	18.4	18.5
9M521	HE fragmentation	21	40
9M522	Separating HE fragmentation	25	37.5

The 9P138. It did not have the suspension locks of the BM-21 as evidenced by the presence of stabilizing jacks at the rear of the vehicle. For traveling, the launcher rotated 180 degrees so that the rear of the tubes faced the front of the vehicle. (Dmitry Terekhov)

The BM-21 was first used during the Sino-Soviet border clashes along the Ussuri River. In March 1969, Chinese forces seized Damansky Island at the culmination of a long-running territorial dispute, forcing Soviet border guards to retreat. Fighting escalated as additional forces were introduced on both sides, but the battle was not decided until the Soviets brought their BM-21s into action. Chinese forces were cleared from the island and surrounding area and the Soviets were able to reoccupy their original positions. Other conflicts in which BM-21s played a significant role include those in Afghanistan, Chechnya, Ukraine, Georgia, Syria, and Angola.

BM-21-1 Grad

The BM-21-1 appeared in 1978 and is essentially the same system as the BM-21, but mounted on a Ural-4320 chassis and with the addition of a thin metal shroud over the rear portion of the launch tube array. The metal shroud covers only the motor section of the rockets and provides thermal, rather than ballistic, protection as heating of the propellant affects the rockets' accuracy.

 BM-24, BM-14 AND BMD-20

1: The BM-24. The Soviets' first postwar system, its configuration was very similar to the BM-31 it replaced. Reflecting the Soviet's experience at the very end of World War II that demonstrated the accuracy advantages of spin-stabilized projectiles, they chose to abandon fins entirely for the BM-24's 240mm projectiles. The BM-24 enjoyed a relatively long service life in the Soviet army. During the Six-Day War, Israel found itself facing this weapon and, lacking an equivalent, pressed captured BM-24s into service.

2: The BM-14. As with the contemporary BM-24, the BM-14 used finless spin-stabilized rockets; the Soviets would later revert to an optimal combination of fin and spin stabilization for their rockets. It was the Soviets' first fielded system that used launch tubes rather than rails or frames, which would later become the standard on MRL systems. While much less capable than the BM-21 that replaced it, it found a continuing role as a naval mount on small craft much as the M-8 and M-13 did in World War II.

3: The BMD-20's 200mm rockets had a much longer range than those of the BM-24, but the launcher only carried four weapons. Along with the BM-25, it is one of the lesser-known postwar MRLs. It was not exported widely, but appeared as recently as 2012 in North Korea, where it was also seen on a naval mount.

The BM-21V. It possessed the GRAU designator 9P125. The artillery regiment of airborne divisions contained a battalion of 12 BM-21Vs and 24 resupply vehicles. The resupply vehicle consisted of GAZ-66B with a 9F37V rack in the cargo bed to hold the rockets. (Vladimir Sappinen)

A BM-21PD firing. Externally, it appears virtually identical to the early production BM-21s, being mounted on the URAL-375 chassis and lacking the thermal shield over the launch tubes. The blunt nose of the PRS-60 rocket can be clearly seen. (Ministry of Defense – Russian Federation)

9P138 Grad-1

The 9P138 was adopted in 1976 as a more mobile version of the BM-21 for the artillery regiments organic to motorized rifle divisions and for the naval infantry regiments. Based on the lighter Zil-131 chassis, it had 36 tubes – four fewer than the 40 on the BM-21 – and weighed about 3,000kg less. It also had a lower center of gravity and was easier to load as a result of the reduced height of the launcher. This was made possible by fitting the elevating mechanism into the space created by the removal of the center four tubes at the bottom of the array. The 9P138 was reportedly intended to fire the then-new M28 series of rockets, although subsequent US testing of a captured Iraqi 9P138 and marketing information from the developer revealed it is capable of firing other 122mm rockets as well.

The 9P138 was exported to Ukraine, Belarus, Kazakhstan, Turkmenistan, Uzbekistan, and Iraq.

9P139 Grad-1

The same document establishing a requirement for what would become the 9P138 also called for the development of a tracked version – the 9P139 – that would have been organic to the artillery regiments of tank divisions. At least three different configurations of launcher arrays with either 36 or 40 tubes on the 2S1 self-propelled howitzer chassis were proposed. Several prototypes were constructed, but the design never entered into series production.

BM-21V Grad-V

A variant of the BM-21 for airborne troops, the BM-21V (Vozdushnodesantiy = Airborne), replaced the RPU-14 and offered a number of advantages over it, including longer-range rockets (20km versus 9.8km), increased fragmentation effect of the high explosive warheads, the ability to airdrop the launcher in a loaded configuration, and reduced time to bring the system in and out of action. The BM-21V consisted of a 12-tube launcher mounted on a GAZ-66B truck. For airdropping, the steering column telescoped and the windshield and side window frames could be folded. The roof and rear of the cab were canvas. It has apparently been withdrawn from active service in the Russian Federation.

BM-21PD

The BM-21PD has a specialized mission: the defense of anchorages

and other sensitive waters from midget submarines operating at a depth of 3–200m and combat divers. It fires a blunt-nose, short-range (5,000m maximum–300m minimum) PRS-60 rocket that functions as a small depth charge. Unlike the standard BM-21, it is equipped with a rectifier that enables it to be connected to an external AC power grid and has the ability to receive sonar data for targeting purposes. It entered service in 1980 and, although an export version exists, was never sold abroad.

LEFT: The 2B26. It has only been produced in small numbers to date. (Ministry of Defense – Russian Federation)

RIGHT: The 2B17-1. The satellite antenna for the navigation system can be seen extending above the cab's roof. (Vitaly Kuzmin)

9A51

The first BM-21 variant for general service use by ground forces to represent a major change in capability is the 9A51. The new features included 50 launch tubes, a variable rate of fire to improve accuracy (stabilization jacks were also added to the rear of the chassis), and an electronic fuse setter that allowed the rocket fuses to be set remotely from the launch vehicle's cab.

The 9A51 is part of the 9K59 Prima complex. Two other components of the complex were also significantly improved. A new high-explosive rocket – the 9M53F – featured a separating warhead. As the rocket descends, the warhead detaches from the rocket body and deploys a small parachute. The parachute causes the warhead to impact the ground almost vertically, greatly increasing the area of the fragmentation effect. Unlike other resupply vehicles in the BM-21 family that consist of a simple rack in the back of a cargo truck that required the crew to manually reload the launcher, the 9A51's resupply vehicle has a mechanized rocket handling system. This reduces the time required to completely reload the launch vehicle from 30 to 10 minutes, despite the increased number of launch tubes.

BELOW: The A215 Grad-M is a naval mount for 40 122mm rockets. It equips both landing ships and small gun-armed combatants primarily for engagement of targets on shore, but can be used against enemy vessels. The mount is reloaded through two hatches directly below the launcher and is accomplished by replacing the array of launch tubes on each side as a single unit. It is shown here on a Project 21630 "Buyan" class corvette. (Vitaly Kuzmin)

Although fielded in 1989, series production ended amid the financial problems and defense cutbacks that followed the collapse of the Soviet Union.

2B26

The 2B26 is sometimes referred to unofficially in the western media as the Grad-K. Functionally, it is similar to the BM-21-1 and has the same thermal shroud, but uses the chassis of the Ural-5350, which is replacing the KamAZ-4320

Tornado-Gs in the field. They can be identified by the remote fuse setting boxes at the end of tubes and the box (arrow) beneath the launch tubes containing the launch tube orientation sensor. The sensor is part of the system that enables the launcher to be elevated and traversed from the vehicle's cab. The long wooden crates each contain one 122mm rocket. As with other BM-21 models, the height of the launcher makes it somewhat awkward for the gunner and loaders. Also, the gunner's panoramic telescope, repositioned and relegated to back-up use, is not as easily accessible. As shown here, a typical field expedient solution is for the crew to construct steps from the rocket crates. (Ministry of Defense – Russian Federation)

as the standard 6 x 6 cross-country truck in the army of the Russian Federation. It entered Russian service in 2012 and was recently filmed in combat in the occupied Donbas region of Ukraine.

2B17-1

In the late 1990s work began on an improved version of the BM-21-1 that incorporated some of the same type of automated navigation and fire control functions as found on the US M270 Multiple Launch Rocket System. This new vehicle, identified in 2012, features:

- an on-board fire control computer
- automated, high speed, and secure data transfer equipment
- a system on the launch tube array that displays its orientation to the gunner on a screen located in the cab
- the ability to lay the launch tube array from the vehicle cab and without using external aiming references
- a satellite navigation system and visual display of the launch vehicle's location, giving the vehicle the ability to fire from unsurveyed positions.

These enhancements allow the vehicle to be operated with only three crew members, greatly increase the speed with which the launch vehicle is able to come into action, and eliminate the need for some of the associated support vehicles that would typically be part of the firing unit.

2B17M Tornado-G

The latest and most capable member of the BM-21 family is the 2B17M or Tornado-G. Adopted for series production in 2013, it has all the features of

TOS-1A, 9P140 URAGAN AND BM-21

1: The 220mm TOS-1's primary direct fire role, a thermobaric warhead as the primary rocket payload, and subordination to the chemical troops make it unique among MRLs. Referred to as a "heavy flamethrower," it can destroy troops in cover that would otherwise be out of the reach of other weapons. After its combat debut in Afghanistan, the system apparently went into hiatus for a number of years before being reintroduced as the TOS-1A shown here. It demonstrated its value in urban combat in Chechnya and most recently appeared in both Iraq and Syria in action against Islamic State forces.

2: The 9P140. Another 220mm system, the 9P140 Uragan uses a completely different family of rockets to those of the TOS-1A. Shown here in firing position, the launcher is turned 180 degrees when stowed for travel. Most recently, it has seen combat on both sides in the conflict in eastern Ukraine. It will be replaced by a new system, the Uragan-1M, on a more modern chassis and will feature easily reloaded pods containing the rockets.

3: The BM-21. The world's most widely fielded MRL. Easy to use and maintain and devastatingly effective, the BM-21 and its associated rockets have undergone numerous upgrades over its more than 50-year history. In its latest iteration, it is as capable as any other medium MRL in service today. Rare for an artillery system, the BM-21 has iconic status as a symbol of Soviet and Russian military power and influence, much like the famous AK-47 rifle.

1

2

3

A 9T452 resupply vehicle reloads a 9P140. The resupply vehicle uses the same ZiL-135 chassis as the 9P140 and is equipped with racks for 16 220mm rockets and a crane for handling the heavy rockets. (Author)

the 2B17-1 and also a remote fuse setting system that electronically applies the correct fuse setting to the rockets before they leave the launch tubes. The Tornado-G is claimed to be three times as effective as the original BM-21.

9P140 Uragan (Hurricane)

Conceptual work on a new heavy MRL began in the early 1960s and development work on what would become the 220mm Uragan began in 1968. During the concept phase, the MT-S tracked transporter was envisioned as the transport vehicle portion of the system, but the developers ultimately selected the high-mobility wheeled ZiL-135 chassis instead. Following State acceptance testing, it entered service in 1975, replacing both the BM-24 and BMD-20.

The 9P140 is based on a modified ZIL-135LMP truck chassis. This 8 x 8 vehicle has superb cross-country mobility, but has an expensive and difficult-to-maintain propulsion system. There are two gasoline engines, transmissions, and drive trains, each powering one side of the vehicle.

The turntable-mounted launcher at the back of the chassis consists of 16 tubes and is traversed to the rear for travelling. The launch tubes have a spiral grove that imparts a stabilizing spin to the rockets, can be elevated from 5 to 55 degrees, and can traverse 30 degrees to either side for firing. The gunner's panoramic telescopic sight, traverse and elevation controls are mounted on the left side of the launcher. The gunner has a small work platform with a short ladder to facilitate access.

The bi-caliber Uragan-1M. The 220mm rocket pods mounted here can easily be distinguished from the 300mm pods by the larger number of missiles in each rocket pod – 15 rather than six – and the chamfer along the top edge of the pods. (www.topwar.ru)

It has a crew of six: commander, driver, gunner, and three assistant gunners. The fiberglass crew compartment contains the usual firing controls and metal shutters protect the windshield during firing. In addition to the launch vehicle and rockets, the other unique part of the 9K57 complex is the 9T452 resupply vehicle. The 9T452 uses the same chassis as the launch vehicle and carries 16 rockets. Once the resupply vehicle is aligned with the launch vehicle, the on-board crane is used to transfer a rocket to a loading rail and a mechanical rammer pushes the rocket into the launch tube.

The following rockets are available for the 9P140:

Designation	Warhead Type
9M27F	HE-fragmentation (Unitary)
9M27K	Fragmentation (Cluster – 30 AT/AP submunitions)
9M27K2	AT mine (Cluster – 24 PTM-1 1.5kg pressure activated mines)
9M27K3	AP mine (Cluster – 312 PFM-1 mines)
9M27S	Incendiary
9M51	Thermobaric
9M59	AT mine (Cluster – 9 PTM-3 5kg magnetically activated mines)

In addition to the spin during launch, folding fins at the rear of the rocket also provide stabilization. All the rocket types have a maximum range of 35km (except the 9M51, which has 13km) and a minimum range of 10km, although this can be shortened to as little as 8km to 9km through the use of an aerodynamic brake ring mounted behind the fuse, similar to those available for 122mm rockets. The rings also help maintain a more consistent circular impact pattern for the salvo regardless of range. A single volley of 16 rockets covers an area of 43 hectares.

All 16 rockets can be fired in half-second intervals. There is also a "ragged" volley mode in which the first eight rockets are fired at half-second intervals and the remainder at two-second intervals. This produces a smaller impact area by reducing the effect of the launcher's oscillation on the final eight rockets.

The 9P140 is normally an Army- or Military District-level system. Like the BM-21, it has seen extensive combat use, having seen action in Afghanistan, Chechnya, the 2008 Russian invasion of Georgia, Syria, and on both sides of the conflict in eastern Ukraine.

Foreign users of the system include Angola, Tanzania, Guinea, Afghanistan, Belarus, Kazakhstan, Syria, Turkmenistan, Tajikistan, Moldova, Peru, Ukraine, Uzbekistan, and Yemen.

In the late 1990s, it was proposed that the aging Zil-135 chassis be replaced with the more modern 6 x 6 BAZ-69092, but this was not taken up. Similarly, Russia experimented with a new version of the 9P140, nicknamed Uragan-1, on the 8 x 8 BAZ-6950, but apparently this also never entered service.

The newest launch vehicle carries the GRAU designator 9A53 and is referred to as the Uragan-1M. The complex designator is 9K512. Although the BAZ-6910 was proposed as the chassis, photographs of the launch vehicle in testing show it based on the Belorussian MZKT-7930. Use of the MZKT-7930 chassis is a logical choice, as it allows the Russian Federation to reduce the number of truck types it operates, the chassis already being in service as the

The TOS-1 in Afghanistan. The box containing the 30 launch tubes is chamfered at the top, making it easy to distinguish from the later TOS-1A. (Author)

G 9A52 SMERCH

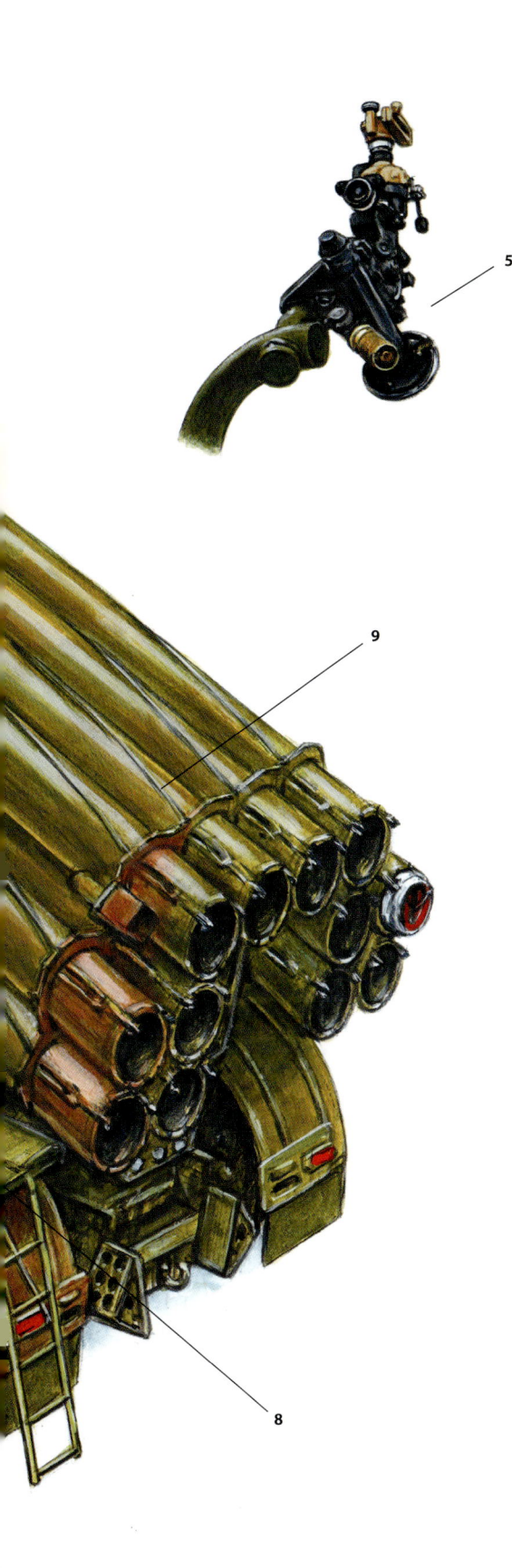

KEY

1. Driver's seat
2. Commander's seat
3. Gunners' compartment
4. Equipment and tool box
5. Gunner's optical sight
6. Stabilizing jack
7. Traversing and elevating mechanism
8. Gunner's platform
9. Spin stabilization groove
10. Remote fuze setter

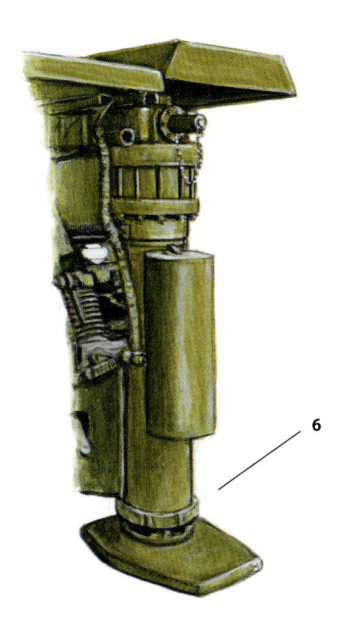

A TZM-T, the resupply vehicle for the TOS-1A. It replaced the unarmored KrAZ-255B-based transloader used with the TOS-1, providing mobility and protection comparable to the launch vehicle. Here the TZM-T's crane had been used to remove one of the lightly armored covers. The rocket racks, colloquially known as "wine racks," are held in place by chains. During reloading the chains are removed and the racks progressively dismantled as the heavy rockets are loaded into the launcher with the assistance of the crane. (Vitaly Kuzmin)

platform for the Iskander ballistic missile system, Bal-E, Bereg, and Bastion coastal defense missile systems, and other applications.

In a departure from all its predecessor MRL systems, it has two sealed rocket pods, each with 15 220mm rockets of the type used by the 9P140. Reloading is accomplished by replacing the entire pod, which greatly reduces the time required for the process compared to reloading individual rockets. In addition, as with the later versions of BM-21, all the navigation, aiming, and other fire control functions are automated and performed from the launch vehicle's cab with a reduced crew. This greatly reduces both the time required to conduct a fire mission after the launch vehicle comes to a halt and the launch vehicle's vulnerability to counter battery fire.

TOS-1 Buratino (Pinocchio)/TOS-1A Solntsepek (Sun)

Designed and produced by the Omsk Transport Machine Factory (OmskTransMash), the TOS-1 (Tyazhyolaya Ognemyotnaya Sistema = Heavy Flamethrower System), was intended to attack troops in the open or in field fortifications, buildings, and lightly armored vehicles at short range.

It is unique among MRLs in that it was designed as a direct fire system and is operated by NBC (Nuclear, Biological and Chemical) defense rather than artillery units. It replaced the OT-55 flamethrower tank in 1988. The original version, the TOS-1 Buratino, was produced only in small numbers for test and evaluation purposes, although it did see combat service in Afghanistan and Chechnya.

The 220mm rockets were fitted with thermobaric or incendiary warheads. Although the same diameter as those fired by the 9P140 Uragan, they had a very different shape and composition. The rockets had a relatively short motor and long payload section as well as a blunt nose that both maximized the volume of the warhead and acted as a de facto airbrake. They had a maximum range of only 3,500m and a minimum range of 400m. The rockets could be fired singly, as "doubles" in which a second rocket is fired nearly

A battery of TOS-1As fires "doubles." It has been exported to Iraq where they are being used against the forces of the Islamic State, Azerbaijan, and Kazakhstan. Exported launchers and resupply vehicles are based on the T-90 rather than T-72 chassis. (Ministry of Defense – Russian Federation)

simultaneously, or as a variable number of rockets in a salvo. Thermobaric warheads produce a fuel-air mixture that when ignited results in a large, extremely hot, explosion with a blast effect of much longer duration than that of conventional explosives. The effect is particularly potent against troops in enclosed areas such as bunkers or buildings.

The short range of the rockets and the direct fire role mandated a launcher that offered more protection than could be offered by a wheeled or lightly armored chassis. Accordingly, the Soviets chose a modified T-72 chassis as the basis for the launcher, designated simply "BM." A commander, gunner, and driver comprised the three-man crew. On the chassis was mounted a low turret in which was seated the commander on the right and the gunner on the left. On top of the turret was a lightly armored pod of 30 launch tubes. The resupply vehicle was unarmored, consisting of a KrAZ-255B truck equipped with a crane, loading rail, and racks for holding 30 rockets.

In the late 1990s, the TOS-1 was modernized, becoming the TOS-1A Solntsepek (Sun). The principal features of the TOS-1A were longer rockets with an extended but still short range of 6,000m, lengthened launch tubes to accommodate the new rockets, a reduction in the number of launch tubes from 30 to 24, and a new resupply vehicle. The TOS-1A system consists of the BM-1 launcher, two resupply vehicles (all mounted on the T-72 chassis), and rockets.

Given its direct fire role, it possesses a laser rangefinder in addition to the gunner's optical sight, cant and level sensors, and a digital ballistic computer that automatically calculates the firing solution and applies the appropriate elevation. It also has multiple navigation systems, including satellite. All combat operations can be conducted without the crew leaving the vehicle. The launcher can come into action 90 seconds after coming to a halt and leave 50 seconds after firing.

The TOS-1A resupply vehicle also uses the T-72 chassis, allowing it to match the mobility and protection of the launcher. It carries 24 rockets in two racks of 12 each with a lightly armored cover that protects against shell

The 9A52-2. The launch vehicle commander sits immediately behind the driver. Behind them and the engine is the gunner's compartment containing the firing controls. Visible here are the access ladder stored across the front of the vehicle, the boxes at the muzzle end of the launch tubes that contain the electronic fuse setters, and the spiral grooves along the length of the tubes that are used to spin the rockets. (Vitaly Kuzmin)

fragments and 7.62mm armor piercing ammunition during transport. To reload, the covers are removed and a loading tray is aligned with one of the launch tubes. The storage racks are progressively dismantled and a rocket lifted by using a hydraulic crane mounted between the pods and lowered onto the loading tray. The rocket is then manually loaded into the tube. It also carries 400 liters of bulk fuel to refuel the launch vehicle.

The primary tactic, pioneered in Afghanistan during 1988 and 1989, is to advance to a firing position, launch a salvo of rockets, and quickly withdraw. During that conflict, the three tubes on each side of the launcher box were left empty to provide an additional measure of protection. The TOS-1 later saw use in the Second Chechen War, where it reportedly achieved results unobtainable from any other system. Most recently, the TOS-1A was observed in the part of eastern Ukraine controlled by Russia and its separatist proxies and in Syria.

9A52 Smerch (Whirlwind)

Adopted for service in 1987, the 9A52 was the answer to the Soviet requirement for a long-range rocket launcher capable of engaging a wide range of targets, including infantry in the open and in field fortifications, soft-skinned vehicles, light and heavy armored vehicles, field and air defense artillery, helicopters in landing zones, and command and control infrastructure. Fielded shortly after the US M270 Multiple Launch Rocket System, the 9A52 fired rockets with over twice the range, although it lacked the M270's rapid reload capability and advanced navigation and fire control systems. The complete complex is the 9K58.

The 9A52 launch vehicle used the MAZ-79111 chassis and its 9T234 resupply vehicle the MAZ-79112 chassis. Although never an official designation, it is sometimes referred to outside the Russian Federation as the BM-30. Jacks between the third and fourth wheels on each side stabilize the launch vehicle during firing.

Twelve 300mm launch tubes are located at the rear of the chassis. In their usual position at the left rear corner are the gunner's work platform, a panoramic sighting telescope, and traverse and elevation controls. A spiral groove in each tube provides a stabilizing spin to the rocket. The array has an elevation from 0 to 55 degrees and can traverse 30 degrees to either side. A single volley covers a target area of more than 67 hectares.

The resupply vehicle carries 12 rockets. As with the Uragan, it is aligned with the launch vehicle for reloading, and the rockets are transferred using the on-board crane to the loading rail, which is equipped with a rammer that pushes the rocket into the launch tube. The process is relatively slow and a complete reload takes about 35 minutes.

The rockets have a course correction system in the form of an on-board gas generator system and vents at the top of the rocket body, which reportedly provide an increase in accuracy of 2 to 3 times compared to unguided rockets, and limit the dispersion of the warheads to 0.25 percent of the range, comparable to that of cannon artillery projectiles.

The basic family of rockets has a range of 70km (20–25km minimum range) and includes the following types:

Designation	Warhead Type
9M55F	Separating HE fragmentation
9M55K	Fragmentation (Cluster – 72 submunitions)
9M55K1	AT (Cluster – 5 IR homing Motiv-3F anti-tank submunitions)
9M55K3	AP mine (Cluster – 64 POM-2 mines)
9M55K4	AT mine (Cluster – 25 PTM-3 5kg magnetically activated mines)
9M55K5	AP/AT (Cluster – 646 or 588 dual-purpose submunitions)
9M55K6	AT (Cluster – 5 IR homing 9N268 submunitions)
9M55K7	AT (Cluster – 20 IR homing 9N282 submunitions)
9M55S	Thermobaric

Uragan-1M with pods for 300mm rockets. It includes the same type of advanced features found on the US M270 and M142 High Mobility Artillery Rocket System (HIMARS). (www.topwar.ru)

A series of 90km rockets using a new propellant – many with the same warheads as the 70km rockets and including new types such as a reconnaissance UAV payload – were also developed.

Designation	Warhead Type
9M528	HE fragmentation
9M525	Fragmentation (Cluster – 72 submunitions)
9M526	AT (Cluster – 5 IR homing Motiv-3F anti-tank submunitions)
9M527	AT mine (Cluster – 25 PTM-3 5kg magnetically activated mines)
9M531	AP/AT (Cluster – 646 or 588 dual-purpose submunitions)
9M533	AT (Cluster – 5 IR homing submunitions)
9M532	AT (Cluster – 20 IR homing submunitions)
9M529	Thermobaric
9M530	HE (Earth Penetrator)
9M534	Reconnaissance UAV

A rocket with a range of 120km, the 9M452, was created for an export customer by increasing the amount of propellant and reducing the size of HE-fragmentation warhead.

A modernized version of the launch vehicle, the 9A52-2, appeared in 1989. A change in chassis to the MAZ-543M for the launch vehicle and MAZ-543A for the resupply vehicle is the primary identification feature of the 9A52-2. The newest version is the Tornado-S. It includes new fire control and communications equipment and an automated fire control system that works in conjunction with the Vivary 1K123 or MP32M1 Slepok-1 command post vehicles. It provides for the secure reception of targeting data, autonomous navigation and positioning of the launch vehicle, and laying of the launcher without the crew having to leave the vehicle. Russia claims that new guided rockets with a range of 120km will be available for the Tornado-S.

The developmental bi-caliber Uragan-1M can carry six 300mm rockets in each of its two pods. It also possesses the same advanced automated satellite navigation and position system, laying, and fire control functions.

Developed for the export market and delivered to India in 2008, the 9A52-2T is essentially the same system as the 9A52-2, but based on the more modern Czech 10 x 10 Tatra 816 chassis, which India produces under license. Its resupply vehicle, the 9T234-2T, is based on the same chassis.

The 9A52-4 is aimed at customers who want a cheaper, more mobile system, but do not require the firepower provided by a 12-tube launch vehicle. There are two options for the six-round launch vehicle, one with the more typical array of reloadable launch tubes. This version is accompanied by the 9T234-4 resupply vehicle that has the usual handling crane, racks for holding rockets, and loading rail. The other version uses a sealed pod with six rockets much like the Uragan-1M. The launch vehicle also has the same autonomous satellite navigation and positioning, laying, and fire control systems that allow the crew to be reduced to two. Both the 9A52-4 and 9T234-4 use the chassis of the 8 x 8 KamAZ-6350.

In addition to Russia, the following countries use one or more of the launchers in the 9A52 family: Belarus, Ukraine, Azerbaijan, Turkmenistan, Kazakhstan, Georgia, Peru, Venezuela, Algeria, Kuwait, the UAE, and India.

The 9A52-4. The example shown here has the sealed rocket pods that expedite the reloading process. (Vitaly Kuzmin)

ASSOCIATED EQUIPMENT

Like other artillery units, those equipped with MRLs are dependent on specialized equipment to provide meteorological input, calculate firing solutions, orient and control the fire of multiple launchers, and perform command and observation functions. Even the most modern MRLs that can perform a number of these functions independently require some degree of external support.

The ability to determine precisely the coordinates, distances, direction, and other mapping-related functions is vital. The 1T-2M topographic survey vehicle addresses this need.

The first set of artillery command and control vehicles was the 1V17, consisting of four different vehicles. The externally identical 1V18 and 1V19 are the command vehicles for the battery and battalion commander respectively; the vehicle's turret houses observation devices and a laser rangefinder. The 1V110, based on the GAZ-66, is the battery fire direction

While local meteorological conditions can be measured directly at the launch site, obtaining important data on the upper air conditions that the rocket will encounter on its trajectory is the function of the RPMK-1 Ulybka. It measures wind direction and speed, relative humidity, temperature and pressure. This data is collected by radiosondes – small instrumentation packages that emit radio signals – carried aloft by balloons. The wind speed and direction can also be determined if necessary by tracking the balloons with the system's radar. The RPMK-1 set consists of the three components shown here: a Ural-4320 with radar and other operational equipment, a Ural-4320 support vehicle with generator and a trailer that carries cylinders of hydrogen gas for the balloons. (Ministry of Defense – Russian Federation).

center and mounts an aiming circle used in orienting the individual launchers. The larger ZiL-131-based 1V111 is the battalion fire direction center.

The 1V126 set supplanted the 1V17 and has only two vehicle types; the 1V152 command and observation vehicle for battery and battalion commanders and the 1V153 fire direction center.

The 1K123 Vivary is the command vehicle set that is part of the 9K58 Smerch complex and is designed to control brigade-size units.

Most recently, the MP32M1 unified command post vehicle, part of the 9S729M1 Slepok-1 complex, was introduced as a replacement for the 1K123.

SELECTED BIBLIOGRAPHY

Foedrowitz, Michael, *Stalin Organs – Russian Rocket Launchers*, Schiffer, Atglen (1994)

Gruntman, Mike, *Blazing the Trail – The Early History of Spacecraft and Rocketry*, American Institute of Aeronautics and Astronautics, Reston (1954)

Kuznetsov, Konstantin, *Reaktivnoe Oruzhie Vtoroi Mirovoi*, Eksmo, Moscow (2010)

Makarov, Mikhail, *Reaktivnaya Artilleriya Krasnoy Armii 1941–1945*, Strategiya KM, Moscow (2005)

Manson, M.P., *Guns, Mortars, and Rockets*, Brassey's, London (1997)

Morozow, M. and M. Kolomiets, *Katiusza: Sowieckie Wojska Rakietowe 1941–1945*, Tank Power 248, Wydawnictwo Militaria, Warsaw (2006)

Shirokorad, A., *Otechetvennye Minomety i Reaktivnaya Artilleriya*, AST, Moscow (2000)

Shirokorad, A., *Entsiklopediya Otochestvennogo Raketogo Oruzhiya 1817–2002*, AST, Moscow (2003)

www.bastion-karpenko.ru
www.epizodsspace.airbase.ru
www.militaryrussia.ru
www.nauka-tehnika.com.ua
www.rbase.new-factoria.ru
www.topwar.ru

INDEX

Note: locators in **bold** refer to illustrations and captions. All military hardware listed is Soviet/Russian unless otherwise stated.

1T-2M topographic survey vehicle 45

accuracy 4, 5, 9, 28, **28**
advantages over guns 4
armored train launchers 13
artillery command and control vehicles 45–46
attack at Orsha **C(18)**19

batteries 17, 20–21
battle of Berlin, the **D(22)**23
battle of Stalingrad, the 21, 22
British adaptation of Indian rocket launchers 4–5

chassis
    4x4 GAZ-63/63A 26
    Chevrolet G-7171 **12**, 24
    GAZ-AAA truck chassis 12
    MAZ-79111 42
    MZKT-7930 37–40
    STZ-5 8, **8**
    Ural-4320 29, 30
    ZiL-135 **36**, 36, 37
    ZiS(ZiL)-151 14, 24, 26
Chechen conflict, the **D(22)**
Chinese use of rocket launchers 4
conflict in Ukraine 22–24, **29**, **F(34)**
Congreve, Sir William 5
Creation and Development of Rocket Artillery in the First Phase of the War (article) 21–22

density of MRL artillery along the front 18
design flaws 12, 13
designator formats for MRLs 7, 8, 37
Directive 002490 on the use of rocket launchers 20–21

evolution of 122mm MRLs 28
exports 21, 25, **25**, 27, 28, 37, 41, 44, 45, **E(30)**

fin stabilization 6, 7, 13, 24, 26, 27, 29, 37, **E(30)**
Flerov, Capt. Ivan 20, **C(18)**19
fragmentation effect 8

GAU (Main Artillery Directorate), the 7, 28
GDL (Gas Dynamics Laboratory) 5–6
GIRD (Group for the Study of Jet Propulsion) 5–6
GRAU (Main Rocket and Artillery Directorate), the 7
Guards mortar battalions 16–17
Guards Mortar Regiments 16, 22

Hale, William 5

industrial designator format 7

KARST-1 (Short Rocket Artillery System for Tanks-1) 5
"Katyusha" nickname 10
Kingdom of Mysore, the 4
Kompleks 6

launch rails 7, 8–9, 12–13, 14, **B(14)**
Lend-Lease program, the 8, 13

M-8-24 mount 12
M270 Multiple Launch Rocket System (US) 34, 42
M1910/1930 howitzer 16, **C(18)**
manual loading 10
meteorological functions 45, **46**
mobility problems 12
Mongol Empire, the 4
MRL artillery units 21
    7th Guards Mortar Division 17
MRLs (multiple rocket launchers) 4, 6, 7, **D(22)**23
    see also rocket launchers
MU-2 prototype 7–8

naval rocket launchers
    16-M-13 deck mount 9, **9**
    24-M-8 20
    A215 Grad-M mount 33
    M-8-M 20
    M-13-M1 9
    M-13-M2 9
nicknames 10, **16**
NII-3 (Scientific Research Institute-3) 6–7

oblique vent holes 9
organizational changes of MRL artillery units 16–17, 21
origins of the rocket launcher 4–5

performance 8–9, 10, 12, **17**, 26, 27–29, 32, 33, 36–37, 40–41, 43
portable mounts 13
postwar MRL development 24–28, **25**
primary targets 18
production 8, 12, **17**, 17–18, **28**, **B14**
projectile specifications **14**, 25
propellant use 5, 6, 9, 16, 25, 27–28, 30, 44
prototypes **6**, 7, 9, 12

range 4, 5, 7, 8, 9, 10, 12, 13, **14**, **25**, 27–28, 40, **A10**, **B14**
Red Army, the 22
reloading 6, 7, **24**, 28, 33, **33**, 36, 40, 43, 45, **D(22)**23, **F(34)**
resupply vehicles 6, 7, 17, 29, **32**, 33, **40**, 41, **41**, 44
    9T234 resupply vehicle 42, 43
    9T452 resupply vehicle **36**, 36
    GAZ-66B truck 26, 32, **32**, 45
    Ural-375D 28, 29
RNII (Jet Propulsion Scientific Research Institute) 6–7
rocket launchers
    2B17-1 **33**, 34
    2B17M (Tornado-G) 34, 34–36
    2B26 **33**, 33–34
    9A51 33
    9A52 Smerch **42**, 42–44, **43**, **44**, **G38–39**
    9A52-2 Smerch 44
    9A52-2T Smerch 44
    9A52-4 Smerch 45
    9P138 Grad-1 **30**, 32
    9P139 Grad-1 32
    9P140 Uragan **36**, 36–40, 37, **F(34)**35
    9P140 Uragan-1M **43**, 44
    16-M-13 9
    A-22 Ogon 26
    BK-1125 armored gunboat **B(14)**15
    BM-8 10–11, 12, 17, 22
    BM-8-8 13
    BM-8-24 12, **12**, 13, 14, **B(14)**15
    BM-8-36 **16**, 16, **B(14)**15

BM-8-48 12, 24
BM-8-72 13
BM-13 **6**, 7, 8–9, 10, 12, 16, 17, 20, **C(18)**19
BM-13 on STZ-5 **A10–11**
BM-13N 8, **8**, 9, 10, 24, **A10–11**
BM-13SN 9, **10**
BM-14 **25**, 25–26, **E(30)**31
BM-14-17 26, 27
BM-14-17M 26
BM-21 24, 28–30, **29–30**, 34, **F(34)**35
BM-21-1 30–32, 33, 34
BM-21PD **32**, 32–33
BM-21V 32
BM-24 21, 24, 24–25, **E(30)**31
BM-25 Korshun 27–28, **28**
BM-31-12 14–15, **16**, 17, 24, **A10–11**, **B(22)**23
BMD-20 27, **27**, **E(30)**31
RPU-14 26, 32
TOS-1 37, 40, 40–41, 42
TOS-1A 41, 41–42, **F(34)**35
rocket specifications
    for 9A52 Smerch 43, 44
    for 9P140 37
    for BM-14 26, 26–27
    for BM-21 29–30
    for BM-24 25
rockets
    9M53F 33
    M-13 7, 8, 9, **14**
    M-13DD 8–9
    M-13UK 9, **14**
    M-20 8, 9, **14**, 21
    M-28 **13**, **14**
    M-30 13–14, **14**, 16, **17**, 17, 21
    M-31 **14**, 14, 16, **17**, 17
    M31-UK **14**, 16
    MD-20F 27
    MS-24UD **25**, 25
    RS-82 6
    RS-132 air-to-ground rocket 6
Rokossovsky, Lt-Gen. Konstantin 20
rotary rocket patent 5
RPMK-1 Ulybka 46
RSZO (salvo fire rocket system) 6
Russian rocket programs 5–7
RVGK (Reserve of the Supreme Command) 16

self-propelled ground MRLs 7
Six-Day War, the 21, 25, **E(30)**
specialized equipment for MRLs 45–46, **46**
spin stabilization 9, 14, 24, 25, 28, 36, 43, **E(30)**
standardization of launchers for chassis 8
Stavka, the 20–21
Studebaker US6 truck (US) 6, 14, 24, **A10**
support role of MRL units 21–22, **D(22)**23

tactical use 18–20, 42
testing 7, 12, 40
thermobaric warheads 40–41
tracked versions 6, 8, **A(10)**11, 12, **B(14)**15, 24-25, 32
TZM (Transporter-Reloading Vehicle) 6

UAV payload for reconnaissance 44, **44**

World War II 20–22, **D(22)**23

ZiS-6 prototype **6**, 7, 12